WHEN FEAR MEETS *Faith*

AUBREY COLEMAN

Study Suggestions

We believe that the Bible is true, trustworthy, and timeless and that it is vitally important for all believers. These study suggestions are intended to help you more effectively study Scripture as you seek to know and love God through His Word.

SUGGESTED STUDY TOOLS

A Bible

A double-spaced, printed copy of the Scripture passages that this study covers. You can use a website like *www.biblegateway.com* to copy the text of a passage and print out a double-spaced copy to be able to mark on easily

A journal to write notes or prayers

Pens, colored pencils, and highlighters

A dictionary to look up unfamiliar words

HOW TO USE THIS STUDY

Begin your study time in prayer. Ask God to reveal Himself to you, to help you understand what you are reading, and to transform you with His Word (Psalm 119:18).

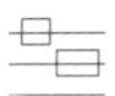

Before you read what is written in each day of the study itself, read the assigned passages of Scripture for that day. Use your double-spaced copy to circle, underline, highlight, draw arrows, and mark in any way you would like to help you dig deeper as you work through a passage.

Read the daily written content provided for the current study day.

Answer the questions that appear at the end of each study day.

The inductive method provides tools for deeper and more intentional Bible study. To study the Bible inductively, work through the steps below after reading background information on the book.

1

OBSERVATION & COMPREHENSION
Key question: What does the text say?

After reading the daily Scripture in its entirety at least once, begin working with smaller portions of the Scripture. Read a passage of Scripture repetitively, and then mark the following items in the text:

- Key or repeated words and ideas
- Key themes
- Transition words (I.e.: therefore, but, because, if/then, likewise, etc.)
- Lists
- Comparisons and contrasts
- Commands
- Unfamiliar words (look these up in a dictionary)
- Questions you have about the text

2

INTERPRETATION
Key question: What does the text mean?

Once you have annotated the text, work through the following steps to help you interpret its meaning:

- Read the passage in other versions for a better understanding of the text.
- Read cross-references to help interpret Scripture with Scripture.
- Paraphrase or summarize the passage to check for understanding.
- Identify how the text reflects the metanarrative of Scripture, which is the story of creation, fall, redemption, and restoration.
- Read trustworthy commentaries if you need further insight into the meaning of the passage.

3

APPLICATION

Key Question: How should the truth of this passage change me?

Bible study is not merely an intellectual pursuit. The truths about God, ourselves, and the gospel that we discover in Scripture should produce transformation in our hearts and lives. Answer the following questions as you consider what you have learned in your study:

- What attributes of God's character are revealed in the passage?

  Consider places where the text directly states the character of God, as well as how His character is revealed through His words and actions.

- What do I learn about myself in light of who God is?

  Consider how you fall short of God's character, how the text reveals your sin nature, and what it says about your new identity in Christ.

- How should this truth change me?

  A passage of Scripture may contain direct commands telling us what to do or warnings about sins to avoid in order to help us grow in holiness. Other times our application flows out of seeing ourselves in light of God's character. As we pray and reflect on how God is calling us to change in light of His Word, we should be asking questions like, "How should I pray for God to change my heart?" and "What practical steps can I take toward cultivating habits of holiness?"

THE ATTRIBUTES OF GOD

ETERNAL

God has no beginning and no end. He always was, always is, and always will be.

HAB. 1:12 / REV. 1:8 / IS. 41:4

FAITHFUL

God is incapable of anything but fidelity. He is loyally devoted to His plan and purpose.

2 TIM. 2:13 / DEUT. 7:9
HEB. 10:23

GOOD

God is pure; there is no defilement in Him. He is unable to sin, and all He does is good.

GEN. 1:31 / PS. 34:8 / PS. 107:1

GRACIOUS

God is kind, giving us gifts and benefits we do not deserve.

2 KINGS 13:23 / PS. 145:8
IS. 30:18

HOLY

God is undefiled and unable to be in the presence of defilement. He is sacred and set-apart.

REV. 4:8 / LEV. 19:2 / HAB. 1:13

INCOMPREHENSIBLE & TRANSCENDENT

God is high above and beyond human understanding. He is unable to be fully known.

PS. 145:3 / IS. 55:8-9
ROM. 11:33-36

IMMUTABLE

God does not change. He is the same yesterday, today, and tomorrow.

1 SAM. 15:29 / ROM. 11:29
JAMES 1:17

INFINITE

God is limitless. He exhibits all of His attributes perfectly and boundlessly.

ROM. 11:33-36 / IS. 40:28
PS. 147:5

JEALOUS

God is desirous of receiving the praise and affection He rightly deserves.

EX. 20:5 / DEUT. 4:23-24
JOSH. 24:19

JUST

God governs in perfect justice. He acts in accordance with justice. In Him, there is no wrongdoing or dishonesty.

IS. 61:8 / DEUT. 32:4 / PS. 146:7-9

LOVING

God is eternally, enduringly, steadfastly loving and affectionate. He does not forsake or betray His covenant love.

JN. 3:16 / EPH. 2:4-5 / 1 JN. 4:16

MERCIFUL

God is compassionate, withholding from us the wrath that we deserve.

TITUS 3:5 / PS. 25:10
LAM. 3:22-23

OMNIPOTENT

God is all-powerful; His strength is unlimited.

MAT. 19:26 / JOB 42:1-2
JER. 32:27

OMNIPRESENT

God is everywhere; His presence is near and permeating.

PROV. 15:3 / PS. 139:7-10
JER. 23:23-24

OMNISCIENT

God is all-knowing; there is nothing unknown to Him.

PS. 147:4 / I JN. 3:20
HEB. 4:13

PATIENT

God is long-suffering and enduring. He gives ample opportunity for people to turn toward Him.

ROM. 2:4 / 2 PET. 3:9 / PS. 86:15

SELF-EXISTENT

God was not created but exists by His power alone.

PS. 90:1-2 / JN. 1:4 / JN. 5:26

SELF-SUFFICIENT

God has no needs and depends on nothing, but everything depends on God.

IS. 40:28-31 / ACTS 17:24-25
PHIL. 4:19

SOVEREIGN

God governs over all things; He is in complete control.

COL. 1:17 / PS. 24:1-2
1 CHRON. 29:11-12

TRUTHFUL

God is our measurement of what is fact. By Him we are able to discern true and false.

JN. 3:33 / ROM. 1:25 / JN. 14:6

WISE

God is infinitely knowledgeable and is judicious with His knowledge.

IS. 46:9-10 / IS. 55:9 / PROV. 3:19

WRATHFUL

God stands in opposition to all that is evil. He enacts judgment according to His holiness, righteousness, and justice.

PS. 69:24 / JN. 3:36 / ROM. 1:18

Creation

In the beginning, God created the universe. He made the world and everything in it. He created humans in His own image to be His representatives on the earth.

Fall

The first humans, Adam and Eve, disobeyed God by eating from the fruit of the Tree of Knowledge of Good and Evil. Their disobedience impacted the whole world. The punishment for sin is death, and because of Adam's original sin, all humans are sinful and condemned to death.

Redemption

God sent His Son to become a human and redeem His people. Jesus Christ lived a sinless life but died on the cross to pay the penalty for sin. He resurrected from the dead and ascended into heaven. All who put their faith in Jesus are saved from death and freely receive the gift of eternal life.

Restoration

One day, Jesus Christ will return again and restore all that sin destroyed. He will usher in a new heaven and new earth where all who trust in Him will live eternally with glorified bodies in the presence of God.

The only One who can truly calm our fears

IS THE ONE WHO WILL EVENTUALLY RID US OF OUR FEARS FOREVER.

TABLE OF *Contents*

WEEK ONE

Day One

INTRODUCTION

SCRIPTURE: PSALM 27:1

When we look at the world around us, we would be hard-pressed to avoid reasons that could lead us to fear. A sin-infested world makes the reality of evil visible to us every day. The news cycle and our social media feeds remind us of the world's brokenness, lest we try to ignore the widespread reality of criminal activity, deadly viruses, political uproar, economic downfall, and the like. Even if we try to remain ignorant to current happenings, fear can be evoked by simply driving in our cars, watching our children at the park, or having a difficult conversation with a friend. Fear is inevitable. It reminds us of our limitations and illuminates our desire for protection. So what should fear look like in the life of a Christian?

Fear is an emotion naturally ingrained in every human being. It is provoked and heightened to varying degrees depending on several circumstances, but we all experience fear in some way. Fear is a gift from God, given for our protection, but how we respond to this emotion is what can make it harmful or helpful. Fear is essentially a concern or hesitation toward someone or something that could cause harm or disrupt our well-being. It can trigger caution in us toward things that are dangerous or pose a threat to us—whether that may be physically, emotionally, or spiritually. It is the feeling we get when we hear an unfamiliar noise in the middle of the night or when a child is too close to boiling water. But it is also the feeling we get when we have said something unkind, and we are afraid of the consequences or when we have to step out of our comfort zone.

Our body can even react to our emotions of fear with a flight or flight response. Though fear can help motivate us to protect ourselves and others, it can also cripple us by leading us away from trusting in the Lord's protection and provision. There is wisdom in exercising caution to the potential dangers that surround us. However, fear can be a tyrant, too. Fear can lead us to resist good and godly things, sheerly because they are unknown and uncertain. Fear can easily motivate us to become anxious about certain scenarios. Fear can dictate our decision-making in a way that keeps us from taking any form of risk. Fear leads us to believe it is up to us to control our circumstances to keep ourselves perfectly out of harm's way. This kind of fear comes from the underlying misbelief that God is not in control or trustworthy. When consumed by fear and anxiety, we may forget God's sovereign and perfect care for us. We may forget He is always in control and worthy of all of our hope and trust. This does not mean all of our fears will fall away when we remember God's faithfulness, but it does anchor our hearts to trust in Him, even amid our fears.

The important question to ask is where our fear leads us. Our feelings of fear will motivate us in one of two directions: toward God or toward ourselves. Either we will lean into the promised assurance and hope we find through salvation in Jesus Christ, or we will cling to our idolized comfort and security, hoping this will lead us safely to the end of our lives. Though protection and precaution are helpful and wise, the latter scenario fails to realize we are limited in our efforts. Our fears are extensive, and we do not always know how to fight them in our own flesh. We do not have all the answers. Even with our best preparations, we cannot keep ourselves from being afraid.

The only One who can truly calm our fears is the One who will eventually rid us of our fears forever. By sending His Son, Jesus Christ, to be crucified on behalf of our sins, God takes our fears and exchanges them for His perfect peace. We face many circumstances that lead us to fear in this life, but Christ has come to bring us peace. Jesus Christ purchased peace with His life to assure us—at every moment and through every circumstance—that there is hope beyond what we see now. We are not left in fear, but instead, we are given the promised hope that all will be right in the world when Jesus returns—fully and finally ridding us of all our fears and restoring peace on earth.

OUR FEELINGS OF FEAR WILL MOTIVATE US IN ONE OF TWO DIRECTIONS:

toward God or toward ourselves.

What makes you most afraid? What do your fears communicate about you?

What underlying misbeliefs about God can you uncover through your fears?

Read Psalm 119:165, Philippians 4:7, 2 Thessalonians 3:16, Psalm 4:8, and John 14:27. How do these verses describe the peace of God? How does the peace of God bring comfort in the midst of our fears?

WEEK ONE

Day Two

"DO NOT FEAR"

SCRIPTURE: ISAIAH 41:10

Throughout Scripture, God's people struggle with fear. This is likely why the Bible mentions fear and being afraid nearly 356 times. Clearly, God had to remind His people over and over again not to be afraid. Even the Israelites, who God rescued out of slavery, continued to fear that God would not give them everything they needed. God continually revealed His promises and purposes to them, yet they still found themselves consumed with fear. We often find ourselves in the same predicament. We know what God says is true, yet we still let fear rule over us. But God did not grow weary in comforting His people then, and He does not grow weary now. God's command not to be afraid is often followed by a heartening proclamation of His promises and presence.

When the word of the Lord came to Abram in Genesis 15:1, God said, "Do not be afraid, Abram. I am your shield; your reward will be very great." God spoke to Joshua in Joshua 1:9 saying, "Haven't I commanded you: be strong and courageous? Do not be afraid or discouraged, for the Lord your God is with you wherever you go." Even when Jesus was born, the angel's birth announcement to the shepherds began with "Don't be afraid, for look, I proclaim to you good news of great joy that will be for all the people" (Luke 2:10). And as John reveals his encounter with the glorified Christ in Revelation, John falls at Jesus's feet like a dead man, and Jesus responds, "Don't be afraid. I am the First and the Last, and the Living One" (Revelation 1:17-18a).

When God's people are instructed not to fear, God often reminds them of who He is and what He has done. He calms their fears with the comfort of His character and promises. He does not simply tell His people not to fear; He gives a reason not to be afraid. This reassurance is offered to us today. No one and nothing can offer us the kind of consolation and peace that Jesus can. He promises to one day rid us of our fears completely, but as we wait for that day, He promises to meet us in them. God promises to be with us, to help us, and to uphold us in times of trouble. He is never taken by surprise. He is our ultimate protector, great and awe-inspiring (Nehemiah 4:14). He has given us all we need to obey, enjoy, and honor Him forever (Matthew 6:33, Philippians 4:19). This means no fear can overtake us, and nothing can rob us of the peace offered to us through salvation in Jesus Christ. Whether we experience fear sending our little ones off to school, being confronted for our faith convictions, or fighting our daily anxieties, God is present with us. He never leaves or abandons us.

The encouragement to hope in God's presence and be comforted by His peace may not be the answers we want to hear when we are afraid. These exhortations may feel like generalized statements invalidating the real and true terrors we face. But God does not simply rescue us from every small thing in this lifetime; instead, He rescues us from this life completely. He saves us from the effects of sin that make fear a reality, and He did this by sending His Son to die on the cross in our place. Through Christ, we can trust that someday we will be free from the effects of sin forever.

If we want temporary solutions to our fear, we can simply look to ourselves, but our protective and precautionary tendencies can only take us so far. Because even with our best intentions, our worst fears can be realized. But God is in the business of everlasting solutions. God's presence does not mean that nothing bad will ever happen to us in this lifetime. However, God does promise that He will use all things for our good and His glory. His presence calls us to hope in a day when sin can no longer run rampant and unruly in our lives. A day when children can run and play with lions, and there will be no fear of harm (Isaiah 11:6-9). A day when man's approval will not affect us because God has ultimately approved of us. A day when murder, enslavement, hatred, sickness, and every perversion of sin will have no place in God's kingdom. No matter what comes our way in a world that taunts us with every reason to be afraid, the only comfort we have as Christians is hope in the presence of the Lord.

GOD DOES PROMISE THAT
HE WILL USE ALL THINGS
for our good and His glory.

When God exhorts His people not to fear, what reminder does He give them? How does the presence of God impact the way we handle our fears?

Read Isaiah 11:6-9. How does this imagery of God's coming kingdom give an idea of the peace to come? How does it comfort you in your fears today?

Write a prayer asking God to remind you of His presence and comfort you with His peace.

WEEK ONE

Day Three

ANXIOUS AND AFRAID

SCRIPTURE: 1 PETER 5:6-8

One of the most common mental illnesses in the world is anxiety. Anxiety is a stress-induced response to feelings of fear or apprehension about what is to come. Anxiety looks different for each person. Anxiety can result in increased heart rate, restlessness, difficulty concentrating, or difficulty falling asleep. It can leave you feeling out of control to such an extent that you struggle to breathe, resulting in an anxiety attack. Whether we possess a genetic predisposition for it or not, anxiety is physical and emotional, and it can affect every part of our being. Lying in bed, our minds can take us back to every flawed moment of our day—what we said, what we did, what someone else said or did—leaving us anxiously assessing every possible scenario, dreaming up outcomes from the most minor to the most catastrophic.

The problem with anxiety is it points us to a future in which we must remain in control and take matters into our own hands. Whether we realize it or not, our anxiety often leads us to remove God completely from the equation. There are truly many reasons to be anxious and afraid. This is a very normal part of our world and is precisely why Scripture speaks to anxiety and fear. God knows this is something we wrestle with in this lifetime. But, when we look to God's Word, we see a message of God's necessary involvement in our anxiety and fears—a message of His love and faithfulness, of His perfect and tender care, and of His near and comforting presence. This is a message that redirects our gaze away from our own efforts and points us toward the opportunity to trust in God.

In order to trust God when we are anxious and afraid, we need humble hearts. The Apostle Peter speaks to a few ways we can fight our anxieties and fears with humility. In 1 Peter 5:6-8, Peter brings the call to "humble yourselves." This is not a passive exhortation but something Christians must actively and continually practice. Humility can be hard, and even when it does not feel genuine, we can pray that God would grant us truly humble hearts through our practice of humility. Humility cultivates a heart posture bent toward God's sovereignty. Peter furthers his teaching by saying we must humble ourselves "under the mighty hand of God," which brings weight and power to His provision and care. God's power and provision are incomparable to our attempts at calming our anxieties and fears. When we try to take matters into our own hands, we assume we are more sovereign and more efficient than God. Without a humble posture toward God's sovereignty, we exalt ourselves, and self-exaltation is not a safe place to be. Our hearts are best kept under His mighty hand, not under our weak ones.

When we remember God's true capabilities, we recognize the futility of our own strength. He brought His people out of slavery; He parted the Red Sea to bring His people through it; He carried His people through the wilderness; He brought His people to the Promised Land; He conquered sin and death by sending His only Son and raising Him from the grave. He is more than capable of bearing the weight of our cares. He delights in doing so. Peter reminds us to cast our cares on God because He cares for us (1 Peter 5:6-8). God's care is extensive with an all-inclusive knowledge of us. God knows our needs before we do, and He can care for our needs better than we can. Our hearts will always cast their cares somewhere, and we must decide who we believe to be our true Savior. Any time we cast our cares apart from Christ, we exalt a false savior in our hearts and minds. Whether we find ourselves turning to ourselves, a trusted friend, or any other source, no one can bear the weight of our cares like Jesus, who willingly took our place on the cross to set us free from sin and bring rest to our weary souls. Why would we cast our cares anywhere else?

When we humble ourselves under the sovereignty of God and rest in His care, we prepare our hearts and minds to remain alert to the schemes of Satan and temptations of sin in this world. The cycle of anxiety can be continual—growing anxious, casting our anxieties, growing anxious, casting our anxieties. If we are not continually relinquishing our anxieties and cares to the Lord, we grow weaker under their weight and weaker in our defenses by the minute. Assuming them for ourselves results in pride, and pride keeps us from running to our capable Savior. Satan loves to attack in our weakest moments. When our minds are consumed with worry and fear, we are far more susceptible to doubt the truth of God's Word and the truth of God's character. We are far more tempted to believe the lies that surface in our greatest fears and most pressing anxieties. But in humility, we are reminded of our incapabilities on our own and our susceptibility to lies. In His goodness, God helps us to willingly run to the only One who can rescue us from all of our hesitations and fears.

OUR HEARTS WILL ALWAYS CAST THEIR CARES SOMEWHERE, AND *we must decide who we believe to be our true Savior.*

In what ways do your fears make you anxious? Who or what do you turn to when you are anxious?

Why must we have humble hearts when we are anxious and afraid? How does humility lead us to position ourselves before God?

Make a list of ways (as many as will fit on the page!) that God specifically cares for you. When you feel most riddled with fear, repeat this practice to serve as a reminder of God's faithful care.

WEEK ONE

Day Four

FEAR OF GOD

SCRIPTURE: PSALM 111:10

The Bible talks about a reverent fear of God that leads us to honor and worship Him in light of His holiness. This is a godly expression of fear, which stems from the belief that God is perfect and mighty and will accomplish His purposes. As we learn more about God, we grow in healthy and reverent fear of who He is. Psalm 2:11 says, "Serve the Lord with reverential awe and rejoice with trembling." This does not mean we are to be afraid of Him, but we are to understand the magnitude of His character in a way that leads us to obey Him, serve Him, and worship Him. This understanding postures our hearts in awe of Him.

God is worthy of all our obedience and praise. And we are called to worship Him with our lives in reverent fear of His worthiness. Through the Bible, we see evidence of God's worthiness. Psalm 89:7 speaks of His worthy distinction, as the psalmist writes, "God is greatly feared in the council of the holy ones, more awe-inspiring than all who surround him." The prophet Jeremiah tells us there is no comparison to God, writing, "Lord, there is no one like you. You are great; your name is great in power. Who should not fear you, King of the nations? It is what you deserve. For among all the wise people of the nations and among all their kingdoms, there is no one like you" (Jeremiah 10:6-7). And in Revelation 4:11, John speaks to God's worthiness to receive all praise, writing, "Our Lord and God, you are worthy to receive glory and honor and power, because you have created all things, and by your will they exist and were created."

With evidence of His worthiness, Genesis 1:26-28 helps us understand our place before a Holy God and how we ought to view ourselves in light of Him. We were created in the image of God, by God, and for God. We were given the privileged role of caring for His creation. We were made to live in perfect fellowship with God, enjoying and delighting in His presence. We were made to live with no shame or fear, in complete freedom and joy in who God made us to be as His image-bearers. Though God created us to be like Him and gave us dominion over the earth, He did not create us to rule over Him. Instead, He desired mankind to represent Him, bearing witness of Him to a watching world and leading others to live in awe of Him.

You may think the worthiness and awestruck wonder of God is a no-brainer, leading you to question why we would ever not fear God. Well, when Adam and Eve's eyes were opened after they sinned in the garden, they immediately covered themselves with fig leaves (Genesis 3:7). This action revealed not only a knowledge of their sin; it also revealed a fear that God would expose them for it. Adam and Eve shifted from a reverent fear of the Lord to a shame-filled fear of exposure. They were no longer full of awe and worship in His presence; they were ashamed in it. They exchanged their awestruck fear of God with the fear of His wrath and judgment. The generations that followed continued to misplace their fear of the Lord with a fear of other things—fear of exposure, fear of man, fear of harm. Each of these fears is filled with traces of the fall of man.

The fall is tragic, and its effects are far-reaching. But it could never deter God's plan of redemption. Jesus Christ came to the world in human form to live in reverent fear of the Lord, modeling a life of worship and doing all things to the glory of God's name. Through salvation, we are no longer enslaved to fear. Jesus has purchased for us a peace that surpasses all understanding, and He has purchased a promise that He will carry us all the way to glory, where the only fear that remains is an awestruck, wonder-filled, worshipful, and reverent fear of the Lord.

A deeper fear of the Lord overshadows every fear of the world. We cultivate a deeper fear of the Lord by meditating on the truth of God's Word and the truth of God's character, by repenting of our pride and tendency toward self-sufficiency, and by preaching to ourselves the profoundly good news of the gospel. Our fear of God leads us to wisely and joyfully trust and obey Him. God alone can carry the weight of our deepest cares and longings, and He alone is worthy of all of our worship.

THROUGH SALVATION,
we are no longer enslaved to fear.

What does it mean to fear the Lord?

Read Psalm 89:7, Jeremiah 10:6-7, Revelation 4:11. Why is God worthy of our fear and worship?

How does our fear of the Lord affect our earthly fears?

Read Psalm 148. In what ways can you practice praise and worship of God in order to grow in reverent fear and awe of Him?

WEEK ONE

Day Five

THOSE WHO FEARED GOD

SCRIPTURE: I THESSALONIANS 2:4

Fear of the Lord in the lives of faithful men and women can look many different ways, and the Bible gives extensive examples. Many people in the Bible lived exemplary lives in fear of the Lord.

In the Old Testament, Noah feared God and obeyed Him by building a giant ark, even when his neighbors likely thought he had lost his mind (Genesis 6:9-22, Hebrews 11:7). Shadrach, Meshach, and Abednego feared the Lord and refused to bow down to false gods, even with the consequence of being thrown in a fiery furnace (Daniel 3:1-23). Esther approached King Ahasuerus for the sake of protecting God's people, knowing her actions could get her killed because she feared the Lord (Esther 5:1-8, 7:1-8:8). Rahab worked to hide Israelite spies, even with the danger of authorities finding out, because she ultimately feared the Lord (Joshua 2, Hebrews 11:31).

In the New Testament, Mary praised the Lord in reverent awe and fear after she conceived the Son of God (Luke 1:46-55). Paul, fearing God, remained a committed and faithful servant who shared the hope and good news of the gospel, even if it meant being despised, beaten, and thrown in jail (Philippians 3:8-9, 2 Corinthians 11:16-33). Peter, who succumbed to fear of man when he denied Christ three times (John 18:15-18, 25-27), eventually filled his writings with exhortations for believers not to fear the things of this world but to trust in God who is supremely worthy of our trust and most worshipful fear (1-2 Peter). Jesus, with death set before Him, feared the Lord and submitted to His ultimate will (Philippians 2:5-8, Hebrews 12:2).

The Bible's history is filled with admirable saints whose fear of the Lord led them to faithful advancement of God's kingdom. But these examples are not just confined to the pages of the Bible. Martin Luther made great strides for the reformation of the church, writing his 95 Theses, which highlighted the Bible as the ultimate authority of the Church because he feared God more than he feared the Catholic Church. Missionaries like Jim Elliot went to the jungles of South America in fear of God, boldly proclaiming the gospel to far-removed tribes, only to be speared to death by them. In fact, there are

Christians all around the world who have been harassed, beaten, tortured, and even killed for their proclamations of faith and pursuits of sharing the gospel to unreached people groups because they feared God more than anything else.

Fearing God in our own lives can look several different ways. Maybe it is a corporate employee standing firm in her faith convictions while knowing she may lose the approval of her manager and coworkers. Maybe it is sharing the gospel with your unbelieving neighbors. Maybe it is avoiding gossip with your closest friends. Maybe it is moving across the country to join a church plant. Maybe it is confessing a hidden sin because you desire God's forgiveness over other people's thoughts of you. From ages of old to the present, fearing God looks like bringing Him honor and praise, listening to and obeying His Word, devoting ourselves to His purposes, walking humbly in His ways, hoping in His promises, loving His statutes, hating evil, and living in awe of who He is and what He has done. What will our lives exemplify? Will our names fit seamlessly on these lists with examples of our faithfulness to the Lord in fear of Him over other things? Or will we find a reverent fear of the Lord does not often take precedence in our life?

However we answer, God remains present and willing to welcome us. Scripture calls us to humble ourselves and turn to the Lord in repentance, and He will readily receive us. We are never too wrecked by our fears. God created us to worship Him, and He is jealous for our worship. He desires our deepest devotion and praise, and He delights in our sacrificial efforts to live righteously for His glory. When we are tempted to be discouraged because the cost of fearing the Lord seems too high, we can be reminded of the ultimate price Jesus Christ paid to redeem our hearts to worship God alone. We owe Him our lives. And we can be encouraged by the many saints before us who gave their lives to the same cause—who, by their faithfulness, brought many to know the awesome wonder of God.

God created us to worship Him,

AND HE IS JEALOUS FOR OUR WORSHIP.

How do the stories of the faithful men and women of the Bible encourage you to fear the Lord?

What does a fear of the Lord look like in everyday life? In what ways do you most commonly struggle to fear the Lord rather than fear man?

God is ready to receive us when we come to Him in repentance. Where do you need to repent from fearing man rather than God?

SCRIPTURE

Memory Verse

THE LORD IS MY LIGHT AND MY SALVATION —
WHOM SHOULD I FEAR?
THE LORD IS THE STRONGHOLD OF MY LIFE —
WHOM SHOULD I DREAD?

PSALM 27:1

Week One Reflection

REVIEW ALL PASSAGES FROM THE WEEK

Summarize the main points from this week's Scripture readings.

What did you observe from this week's passages about God and His character?

What do this week's passages reveal about the condition of mankind and yourself?

How do these passages point to the gospel?

How should you respond to these passages? What specific action steps can you take this week to apply them in your life?

Write a prayer in response to your study of God's Word. *Adore God for who He is, confess sins He revealed in your own life, ask Him to empower you to walk in obedience, and pray for anyone who comes to mind as you study.*

FEAR OF THE LORD

IN THE BOOK OF PROVERBS

The book of Proverbs provides a wealth of wisdom for the Christian. Throughout this book, you will find that wisdom and the fear of the Lord go hand in hand. Read these passages, and summarize how the Bible instructs us to walk wisely in the fear of the Lord.

"The fear of the Lord is the beginning of knowledge; fools despise wisdom and discipline." —Proverbs 1:7

"Because they hated knowledge, didn't choose to fear the Lord, were not interested in my counsel, and rejected all my correction, they will eat the fruit of their way and be glutted with their own schemes." —Proverbs 1:29-31

"My son, if you accept my words and store up my commands within you, listening closely to wisdom and directing your heart to understanding; furthermore, if you call out to insight and lift your voice to understanding, if you seek it like silver and search for it like hidden treasure, then you will understand the fear of the Lord and discover the knowledge of God. For the Lord gives wisdom; from his mouth come knowledge and understanding." —Proverbs 2:1-6

"Don't be wise in your own eyes; fear the Lord and turn away from evil." —Proverbs 3:7

"The fear of the Lord prolongs life, but the years of the wicked are cut short." —Proverbs 10:27

"The fear of the Lord is a fountain of life, turning people away from the snares of death." —Proverbs 14:27

"Iniquity is atoned for by loyalty and faithfulness, and one turns from evil by the fear of the Lord." —Proverbs 16:6

"The fear of the Lord leads to life; one will sleep at night without danger." —Proverbs 19:23

"Don't let your heart envy sinners; instead, always fear the Lord. For then you will have a future, and your hope will not be dashed." —Proverbs 23:17-18

Summary

WEEK TWO

Day One

FEAR OF MAN

SCRIPTURE: PSALM 118:8, PROVERBS 29:25

Bowing to the thoughts, actions, and perceptions of those around us remains a common struggle for many Christians. When we are too concerned with what people think and believe about us, the fear of man can seep into every aspect of our lives. It can shape the way we interact with our co-workers and our bosses in the workplace. It can determine the way we interact with members of our church. It can shape how we respond to our spouses, children, friends, and families. It can even leave us stumbling over our words, changing our convictions, or simply withholding our true opinions. The fear of man can inform our thoughts, our decisions, and our choices. When the fear of man replaces a reverent fear of God, people take greater precedence in our lives than God.

There is not only one kind of person who gives in to the temptation of this fear. The weak and the strong both struggle with the fear of man—the bold and the timid, the rich and the poor, the beloved and the outcast, the believer and the non-believer. Fear of man is a common struggle for many. The main reason we fear man includes the fear that we will be physically hurt, rejected, or exposed by man. These fears can be born out of past experiences that leave us hurt and skeptical. Perhaps circumstances in which we felt abandoned, alone, or rejected cultivate these fears. Our fears can be the product of our pride, leaving us afraid man will crush our ego or make us look bad. These fears can even result from placing unhealthy expectations on others, which leads us to care too much about what people think and say. We may even feel we need or deserve approval and validation to feel secure with ourselves, causing us to fear man.

Maybe we struggle to resonate with the fear of man. We may consider ourselves to be confident, unconcerned with what others think, and unapologetically ourselves. But, we may be surprised at the answers to a few questions intended to help us diagnose the fear of man in our hearts and minds. Have you ever struggled with peer pressure? Do you find it challenging to tell people no? Do you worry others misunderstand you? Do you find it easy to lie to protect how you are perceived? Do you often second guess yourself? Do you find yourself too easily falling into envy or comparison? These are only a few ways we can accurately gauge our inclinations toward the fear of man. Questioning ourselves helps us get to the root cause of each of those scenarios. And even if we feel we are exempt from such fear, we are not, and we must be aware of the temptations that aim to lure us in.

We must also be aware of what the fear of man produces in our lives. When we live outside of the fear of the Lord, the things we fixate our eyes on direct and shape our hearts. When we live for man's approval and acceptance, we will surely produce a life of disappointment and discontentment. We will never be satisfied by their thoughts and opinions. The unhealthy expectations we place on others to perfectly praise, care for, and make us feel secure will only lead to a cycle of unhealthy dependencies and unmet expectations. After continually being failed by man, we may even grow cynical and bitter toward people altogether, isolating ourselves so we cannot be hurt or rejected again.

The Bible reminds us, "The fear of mankind is a snare, but the one who trusts in the Lord is protected" (Proverbs 29:25). The fear of man is easy to fall into but difficult to escape, like a trap that fastens its grip on us and will not let go. These fears attack our identity in Jesus Christ and bring us to question our security in Him. Our fears seek to minimize the astounding reality that because of salvation in Christ, we stand before a Holy God loved and approved. But we have to fight with every fiber of our being and the help of the Holy Spirit to remember that nothing, no rejection or harm or exposure, can separate us from the love of God (Romans 8:38-39). We find protection in the love of the Lord, and we can put our hope and trust in Him.

OUR FEARS SEEK TO MINIMIZE THE ASTOUNDING REALITY THAT BECAUSE OF SALVATION IN CHRIST, WE STAND BEFORE A HOLY GOD *loved and approved.*

Consider the diagnosis questions listed in paragraph three. How did they help you gauge your tendency to fear man?

What does the fear of man produce in our lives? How does it affect our relationship with God? With others?

How does our secured identity in Jesus Christ free us from bowing to the fear of man?

WEEK TWO

Day Two

THOSE WHO FEARED MAN

SCRIPTURE: JOHN 12:43

The Bible is filled with examples of those who fell into the fear of man. We might even be surprised by some of the faithful saints who gave in to the pressures of man. Think about Aaron in the book of Exodus. When Moses went up on the mountain to hear from the Lord after leading the Israelites out of slavery in Egypt, the Israelites began to complain about waiting for him to come back down. They were so discontent that they complained to Aaron about it, even after they had been rescued in such a monumental way. With all of the complaints, Aaron succumbed to the pressure of the people. He collected their gold and fine jewelry and fashioned it into a golden calf for them to worship. He clearly feared man more than he feared God because it seems he did not think twice about it. Even when God sent Moses back down to confront him, Aaron made excuses and defended his actions (Exodus 32).

What about Elijah? God powerfully used him on Mount Carmel, confronting King Arab and Queen Jezebel's institution of Baal worship and proving God is the only One truly worthy of our worship (1 Kings 18). But when news broke that many were turning from Baal worship to worship God, Queen Jezebel was outraged and sent for Elijah to be killed. Elijah was so afraid that he ran as far as possible and found himself under a tree asking God to take his life (1 Kings 19). He had just witnessed God's mighty hand over him, yet he still feared what man could do to him.

Jonah provides a considerable example as well. God commissioned Jonah to go to the Assyrian city of Nineveh and preach against evil. This was significant because the Ninevites—known for their cruelty, military power, and violence—were notorious enemies of Israel. Jonah sought to run away from God's presence because he did not want to go preach to these people. However, after being swallowed by a great fish, Jonah finally followed God's call and went to Nineveh. When the Ninevites heard Jonah's message, they fasted and repented, and the Lord showed mercy to them. Jonah was outraged, revealing his true hesitation from the very beginning—he knew the compassion and mercy of God, and he did not want it to be shown to his enemies, the Ninevites. His fear of man manifested in an unjust hatred toward others.

Looking to New Testament examples, we come to Peter. He was a disciple of Jesus and followed Him closely during His time on earth. But leading up to His death, Jesus predicted Peter would deny Him. Peter was baffled by such a claim, considering his close relationship with Jesus. He could not believe Jesus would say something like that about him. But when the time came, and people started asking Peter if he was associated with Jesus, Peter was overcome with the fear of man and denied knowing Jesus. He did not just deny Jesus once, but he denied Him three times.

The Pharisees, too, feared man in both their words and actions. They conducted themselves in a manner that was outwardly respected by those around them. They seemed to be righteous examples. But they were more concerned with how they appeared before others than how they appeared before God. In Matthew 15:8, Jesus tells us the Pharisees honored God with their lips but not with their hearts. Their greatest concern was to appear upright and honorable to be approved and respected by man.

Each of these examples demonstrates the fear of man manifesting in different ways. We learn what we fear most when we see what we are willing to compromise or give up to protect ourselves. Even those who walked closely with Jesus, who held positions of power, or who were given incredible tasks still fell victim to the fear of man. Not one of us is exempt from this temptation, and this is because of our fallen, sinful nature. In our sin, we look to others for acceptance and approval when we need only look to God.

However, Christ came to save us from sin's power over us. Through Christ's redemption, we are finally freed from all our natural, sinful tendencies and desires—including the fear of man—and we are equipped to walk forward in confidence, trusting Him. When we trust Jesus, God uses our fears to sharpen and strengthen us in our faith. In our weakness, God meets us with His grace, which is always sufficient. Because of this grace, the Apostle Paul can write, "I will most gladly boast all the more about my weaknesses, so that Christ's power may reside in me" (2 Corinthians 12:9). We will all fall to the snares of man. When we do, we can trust God will meet us there—just as He met Aaron, Elijah, Jonah, Peter, and so many others throughout Scripture. God is ever faithful to His people throughout the ages, and we can look to Him when we are afraid.

GOD IS EVER FAITHFUL TO HIS PEOPLE THROUGHOUT THE AGES, AND *we can look to Him when we are afraid.*

Did you resonate with any of the biblical examples of those who feared man rather than God? What do you learn from their stories?

How can God use your fears to sharpen your faith?

What evidence have you seen of this in your own life and the lives of others?

WEEK TWO

Day Three

FEAR OF HARM

SCRIPTURE: PSALM 56

The truth is the fear of man is multifaceted. It can take us in many directions, and sometimes, our fear of man can more specifically come from the fear of being harmed by man. Real and valid terrors confront us in this life, and people can hurt us. We are uncomfortably aware of the potential for us to be harmed, threatened, or oppressed by others. This is precisely why many of us hold our keys between our fingers while walking to our cars at night. It is why sudden noises in dark places leave us frozen. It is why we keep our eyes glued to our children in public and why millions of Americans install security alarms in their homes. So how do we approach this real and valid fear?

Throughout the Bible, we see evidence of those willing to inflict harm even to the point of death—Cain murdering Abel out of jealousy, David murdering Uriah to cover up his own sin, King Herod beheading John the Baptist at the request of a woman who hated John. Unfortunately, we continue to see evidence of this today. Even beyond the heinous act of murder, consider other acts of harm like racism, bullying, or physical, sexual, and emotional abuse. Such experiences can leave us incredibly traumatized and apprehensive about living with peace and comfort in this world. The sin of humanity and the inclination of man's heart to only do evil all the time (Genesis 6:5) seems like a valid reason to feel afraid. Sometimes, fear may feel like the most rational and appropriate response.

While we should be afraid at times, we cannot forget who God is in our fears. There is certainly a level of security and protection that can serve us, and we should not dismiss appropriate safety precautions. But our fear of harm, like every emotion, is going to lead us somewhere. Maybe it leads us to anxiety, paranoia, distrust, control issues, or isolation. It is normal to be afraid of someone harming us, but the truth of God's character must ultimately shape our fears, and they must lead us to a safe and secure trust in Him. Anxious thoughts will only leave us sleepless and worried. Paranoia will only lead us to isolation and distrust. And a desire for control will continually remind us how much is out of our hands. But God is a safe place for us. He is our Divine Protector and our greatest defense against the evils of this world. He knows the deepest hurts people have caused us, even the hurt no one else knows about. He sees the scars and the pain, and in Him, we find lasting refuge and strength.

David spoke the truth of God's character to his soul as he faced the attacks of the Philistines. He proclaimed, "When I am afraid, I will trust in you. In God, whose word I praise, in God I trust; I will not be afraid. What can mere mortals do to me?" (Psalm 56:3-4). Though mere mortals could clearly do a great deal to him, like destroy his kingdom and end his life, they could not kill his soul, and they could not snatch him out of God's hand. David recalled the perfect knowledge of God. He reflected on God's sovereign insight over his life. David took time to consider God in the midst of his fears and concluded, "You yourself have recorded my wanderings. Put my tears in your bottle. Are they not in your book? Then my enemies will retreat on the day when I call. This I know: God is for me" (Psalm 56:8-9). David's fear of harm led him to call on and trust in the Lord. His fears were not eradicated or avoided, but his faith shaped how he handled his fears. His panic turned to praise. David knew who truly held the power of life and death—and we can have this confidence, too.

In the New Testament, Jesus instructed His followers, "Don't fear those who kill the body but are not able to kill the soul; rather, fear him who is able to destroy both soul and body in hell" (Matthew 10:28). Likewise, Jesus did not let the fear of harm keep Him from His ultimate mission on earth. Through His death on the cross, Christ made the ultimate sacrifice on our behalf, freeing us from the fear of harm, once and for all. The Apostle Paul emphasizes this tremendous gift in his letter to the Roman house churches. He reminds these believers that nothing—not even death—can separate us from the love of God that is in Christ Jesus our Lord (Romans 8:31-39).

When we feel vulnerable to harm, we can call on the Lord like David, and we can carry the confidence of Paul. Our God is an ever-present help in times of trouble (Psalm 46:1, NIV). Even if He does not divinely rescue us from the hurt of others in the moment—which He can and does do—He will one day completely rescue from this world all who put their faith and hope in Him. Our trust in Christ brings liberating power to even the most threatening fears. When we are afraid, may we put our trust in Him.

WHEN WE ARE AFRAID,

may we put our trust in Him.

How do you approach the fear of harm? What past experiences have shaped that fear?

What aspects of God's character did David meditate on in Psalm 56? How did each character trait combat His fear?

Why is it important to speak the truth about God to our souls? What practices can you implement into your life that better allow you to remember what is true about God amid your fears?

WEEK TWO

Day Four

FEAR OF REJECTION

SCRIPTURE: 1 SAMUEL 15, JOHN 12:42-43

We pay attention to the "likes" and "comments" on our social media platforms. We are thrilled to receive an invitation to the friend group we long to join. We want to be liked. We want to be included. We want to feel significant and valuable. And it all boils down to the fact that we all crave acceptance and hate rejection. No one enjoys feeling left out, alone, or outcast. To protect ourselves from feeling that way, we cultivate a fear of rejection.

People can reject us. They can make us feel insignificant and unwanted with both their words and their actions. When we experience the sting of rejection, many of us will do anything to keep ourselves from experiencing it again. We might become less vulnerable with people. We might blame-shift to keep negative attention off of ourselves. We might become worrisome, too consumed with what other people are thinking about us. We might manipulate and show favoritism to gain the approval we desire. Our fears can show us where our allegiance lies. When the fear of rejection leads us to place people on a pedestal to avoid rejection, we give them complete power over our lives.

The approval of man is commonly addressed in Scripture because we are so prone to idolize it. We can care too much about what people think because we believe they have the power to give us the purpose and meaning we really want. King Saul is a noteworthy example of one who acted out of fear of rejection. In 1 Samuel 15, God instructed Saul to destroy the Amalekites and all they had. He was not to spare anyone or anything. When the time came, his army wiped out their entire city, except their king and the best of their animals. King Saul did not completely obey the Lord's command. When Samuel confronted him, King Saul made excuses at first, but he eventually confessed that he did not obey God because he was afraid of the people. His fear of man led him to disregard God's commands because he was more concerned with letting people down than God.

At the end of John 12, we find one of the saddest examples of the fear of rejection. At that point in Jesus's ministry, many Jewish leaders secretly believed in Him. They witnessed His signs and wonders. They heard and followed His teachings, yet they did not openly profess their allegiance to Him because they feared the rejection that might come from following Him. These people ultimately loved the praise of men more than they loved the praise of God, and they were not willing to sacrifice it to follow Jesus (John 12:42-43).

Later, after Jesus's arrest, the governor, Pontius Pilate, placed Jesus and a notorious prisoner named Barabbas before a crowd of Jews. Each Passover, it was the governor's custom to allow the Jews to choose one prisoner to be released. When Pilate presented these two options, the crowd chanted to set Barabbas free. Despite knowing Jesus had not committed any crime, Pilate chose to appease the masses, becoming conductor of the greatest mistrial of all time. He feared the displeasure of the people more than he feared God. Therefore, he sent Jesus to the cross to be crucified (Matthew 27:15-26).

How often do we find ourselves in the same position? Maybe we are afraid to share the gospel because we do not want to be shot down. Maybe we fail to live out our Biblical convictions because we do not want others to look down on us. Maybe we shape our faith with our current culture in hopes that we will be more widely accepted. In these ways, we seek the acceptance of man rather than God.

Jesus modeled what it means to live in the assurance of God's acceptance by fearing the Lord faithfully, even to the point of death. He was rejected, despised, beaten, and eventually killed by men because He did not live in fear of man. This begins to put our fear of rejection into perspective. Jesus, the most perfect man to ever walk the face of the earth, experienced the most severe form of rejection. He was the essence of innocence, yet man still conjured up reasons to bring charges against Him. But what man intended for harm, God used for good. Jesus was rejected for us so that we could be accepted by God.

In Ephesians 2, Paul reminds Christians that those in Christ are clothed in His righteousness and can now stand before God, approved and accepted by Him. Jesus's death paid the penalty for our sins and purchased a hope that sets us free from all our earthly fears. Christian, you have received the greatest approval and acceptance you will ever need in Jesus. Because Jesus knew rejection well, He is also able to sympathize when we are rejected (Hebrews 4:14-16). And because Jesus serves as our High Priest, mediating for us, we can come to Him with all of our fears of rejection. We can draw near to Jesus with confidence, asking Him to replace our inadequate fears with a complete and worship-filled fear of God.

WE CAN DRAW NEAR TO JESUS
with confidence

In what ways do you find yourself fearing rejection?

How does the gospel speak to our fear of rejection?

What would it mean to live in light of the One who was despised and rejected by man so that we could have a relationship with God?

WEEK TWO

Day Five

FEAR OF EXPOSURE

SCRIPTURE: JOHN 3:19-21

How often do we find ourselves afraid to ask others for help because we want to appear we have everything under control? How often do we brush harmful patterns and behaviors under the rug, hoping that they will go away? How often do we struggle to share honestly and vulnerably with others? Underlying all of these scenarios is the fear of exposure. We are afraid of being exposed. We are afraid of people seeing the hidden parts of our lives that we have kept in the dark. We fear the responses others might have, the truth that would be brought to light, and the consequences brought forth by such exposure. But from where does this fear come?

In the beginning pages of the Bible, Adam and Eve had everything they could have ever desired. They lived in perfect harmony with God in the garden of Eden. The only thing they did not have access to was the Tree of Knowledge of Good and Evil. God forbade them to eat from it. But when enticed by Satan, they doubted God's goodness and ate from the tree. Instantly, they became aware of their sin. As a result, they hid from God and covered their bodies with fig leaves in shame. They were afraid of being exposed for their sin and disobedience. They were afraid of the consequences caused by their actions. And they were ultimately afraid of being seen and fully known in their rebellion. This fear of exposure has carried through generations, and we, too, are prone to run and hide in our sin. This is the ripple effect of the fall. Freedom is lost. Fear enters in. And we are afraid of being exposed for who we really are.

But where does hiding leave us? Is hiding really better than being exposed? Pretending and saving face can only last for so long if we desire a deep and meaningful relationship with others and an honest relationship with God. Not revealing our truest selves only leads to isolation. Like mold grows best in the dark, our sin will continue to grow if it is not brought to the light. Sin invades, entices, distorts, and devours. And ultimately, sin leads to death. When we fear exposure, we never deal with our sin, leaving us with no room for repentance and change. We should never minimize the temptations of sin or ignore the crafty schemes of Satan. And we certainly should not ignore the consequences of sin being covered up. When concealed, sin will only grow and entangle us more over time, eventually enslaving us to it.

There are moments in life when our sin will bring us to the harsh realization of how broken we are. Our gut reaction might be to hide our faces and run. Our temptation might be to conceal the ugly parts of ourselves so that we can avoid condemnation. However, even if we succeed in hiding our sin from others, our sin is never hidden from God. He knows every facet of our being—our thoughts, our intentions, and our actions. God knows the deepest depths of our sin, and we are even worse than we or anyone else thinks we are. But the gospel frees us from the implications our sin should bring. For the Christian, our sin does not get the final say. God, in His sovereignty, had a plan of redemption all along—a plan to send His Son, Jesus, to die on our behalf, to bear the weight of all the sin that pushes us into the shadows. Jesus rose from the grave three days later so that we too could be raised to walk in the light with Him.

Christ invites us into salvation, seeing all of our faults and flaws fully exposed. The gift of the gospel is offered to all who repent of their sin and put their trust and hope in Jesus. And, to truly repent, we have to confront our sin and bring it to the light. True repentance requires full exposure, and it leads us to see our true need for a Savior. It is in our need that we cry out for rescue. Christ not only saves us, but He invites us in to change us. He calls us in to sanctify us into His likeness. He carries our sin to the cross and clothes us with radiant faces (Psalm 34:5).

Because of Christ, we do not have to be afraid of exposure. The hope of the gospel frees us to live authentically, revealing the best and the worst of ourselves to those around us while pointing to God's redemptive work in our hearts. Why? Because Christ has set us free from sin and given us His righteousness. No one can condemn us or shame us for our sin because Christ bore all our shame and condemnation on the cross. We do not have to pretend to possess a righteousness of our own. We do not have to pretend we do not struggle with sin. Instead, we can confess our hardships, sin struggles, and vulnerabilities to others. We can repent and walk in the forgiveness offered to us in Jesus. We can put on the righteousness of Christ and allow the Spirit to sanctify us more and more to look like Jesus every day.

God knows even the vilest and most detestable parts of our hearts and still chose to send His Son to rescue us from our sins. We do not have to fear exposure. We can lift our eyes with full assurance, running willingly to the One who sees it all and loves us still.

Christ not only saves us,

BUT HE INVITES US IN TO CHANGE US.

How do you see the fear of exposure in your own life? (e.g., Is your private life different from your public life? Are there things about you you do not want anyone to know about? Are there sins you struggle to confess?)

How does fear of exposure affect our ability to repent and seek forgiveness?

How does the gospel set us free from fearing exposure?

SCRIPTURE

Memory Verse

WHEN I AM AFRAID,
I WILL TRUST IN YOU.
IN GOD, WHOSE WORD I PRAISE,
IN GOD I TRUST; I WILL NOT BE AFRAID.
WHAT CAN MERE MORTALS DO TO ME?

PSALM 56:3-4

Week Two Reflection

REVIEW ALL PASSAGES FROM THE WEEK

Summarize the main points from this week's Scripture readings.

What did you observe from this week's passages about God and His character?

What do this week's passages reveal about the condition of mankind and yourself?

How do these passages point to the gospel?

How should you respond to these passages? What specific action steps can you take this week to apply them in your life?

Write a prayer in response to your study of God's Word. *Adore God for who He is, confess sins He revealed in your own life, ask Him to empower you to walk in obedience, and pray for anyone who comes to mind as you study.*

HEART DIAGNOSIS

This week, we learned about three different types of fear—the fear of rejection, the fear of harm, and the fear of exposure. To discern which fears you might be most susceptible to, prayerfully work through the following questions. As you do, pray Psalm 139:23-24, asking the Lord, "Search me, God, and know my heart; test me and know my concerns. See if there is any offensive way in me; lead me in the everlasting way."

FEAR OF REJECTION

- ○ Do you struggle with peer pressure?
- ○ Do you find it difficult to say "no," resulting in overcommitment?
- ○ Do you find yourself placing unrealistic expectations on your spouse, your friends, or your family?
- ○ Are you easily offended or easily embarrassed?
- ○ Do you worry about being misunderstood by others?
- ○ Have you ever been too afraid to identify as a Christian or share your faith?

FEAR OF HARM

- ○ Do you find it difficult to trust others?
- ○ Do you find yourself perceiving someone as unsafe because of how they look, dress, or talk?
- ○ Do you become anxious when you find yourself in unknown and uncomfortable places and circumstances?

- ○ Do you assess the possibility of harm in your normal, everyday activities (e.g., walking around the neighborhood, going to the store, driving, being in public places, etc.)?
- ○ Do you find yourself idolizing comfort?
- ○ Do you find yourself clinging to safety at the cost of disobeying God?

FEAR OF EXPOSURE

- ○ Are you afraid of what people could find out about you?
- ○ Do you find it easy to lie, embellish, or alter certain information about yourself to look a certain way to others?
- ○ Do you easily isolate yourself and avoid others when you are struggling?
- ○ Do you find it easy to cover up and hide your sin?
- ○ Do you find yourself idolizing control over the way you are seen and perceived?
- ○ Do you find it difficult to confess and repent of your sin to God and others?

SEARCH ME, GOD, AND KNOW MY HEART;
TEST ME AND KNOW MY CONCERNS.
SEE IF THERE IS ANY OFFENSIVE WAY IN ME;
LEAD ME IN THE EVERLASTING WAY.

Psalm 139:23-24

WEEK THREE

Day One

COMBATTING FEAR

SCRIPTURE: HEBREWS 13:6

By planting our trust firmly in the Lord, we are equipped to daily combat the lies that fear provokes in us. As we feel threatened by these lies, there are practical ways we can fight our fears. But to fight our fears, we need to understand them. Throughout this study, we have dived deeply into the root causes of specific fears we may find ourselves struggling with. Whether we fear exposure, rejection, or harm, our fears tell us what matters most to us and what we are most afraid of losing. Is it protection? Is it comfort? Is it approval? Our fears serve as flashing indicators of where our hearts and minds are fixated.

Instead of turning away from God when we are afraid, we can turn to Him with our fears. One of our greatest spiritual resources for all of life is prayer. It is a privilege, as Christians, to have access to the Father in prayer. With Jesus Christ as our mediator, we can seek God for help and strength. We can humbly approach Him at any time, and we can never exhaust Him. The more we pray, the more we cultivate a dependency and trust in Him. When we have trouble discerning truth from lies, we can pray and ask God to call to mind the truths of His Word. When we find ourselves in situations that make us more susceptible to fear, we can pray and ask God for strength. When we find ourselves idolizing people's perceptions, we can pray and ask God to turn our eyes away from worthless things and find true delight in Him.

Even if we do not know exactly what to pray, the Spirit intercedes for us in prayer (Romans 8:26-27). There are countless ways we can practice prayer to posture our hearts and minds toward the only One who can truly equip us to face our fears. When we feel anxious about something, we can pause to pray and ask for God's peace. When we find ourselves hesitant or afraid to move forward, we can pray and ask God for courage and strength. Even if we find ourselves falling into sinful responses to fear—like idolizing comfort, reacting in anger and frustration, or consuming ourselves with worry—we can come before the Lord in prayerful repentance. We can ask for His forgiveness. We can name our fears and ask for God's comfort and peace. We can beg Him to bring us a great reverence and fear of Him. What a gift of grace that a Holy God hears the prayers of lowly sinners like us. Not only does He hear us, but He delights in hearing us, and He helps us in every moment of need.

Often when we grow anxious and worried, it is because we are straining our minds too far into the future. We can obsess over hypothetical scenarios and possible outcomes to such an extent that we cannot put one foot in front of the other. But God wants us to remain in the present. In His Word, He instructs us to only consider today because each day has its own trouble (Matthew 6:34), and He reminds us His grace is always sufficient (2 Corinthians 12:9). Daily replacing our fear-filled thoughts with meditations on the truth of God's sufficiency and care can safeguard us from letting our minds wander too far. This grounds our gaze to Him alone and helps us to remain steadfast in times of trouble.

Memorizing Scripture is a powerful weapon in the fight against our fears. God's Word is vital to life and godliness as a Christian. Biblical truths ground us when our fears come to the surface. In his second letter to Timothy, Paul teaches us, "All Scripture is inspired by God and is profitable for teaching, for rebuking, for correcting, for training in righteousness, so that the man of God may be complete, equipped for every good work" (2 Timothy 3:16-17). We are shaped and transformed by the truth of God's Word as we store it up in our hearts and minds. God's Word helps us fight anxiety, people-pleasing, paranoia, and every kind of fear we can conjure. The more we come to know God's Word, the more we come to know God. Through Scripture memorization, we fill our minds with His promises, His character, His love, and His sovereignty to hold us fast amidst our greatest fears.

As we see time and time again, we are prone to wander and forget God. Our greatest danger is not being afraid—it is forgetting God amid our fear. When we rely solely on ourselves to escape, control, or avoid our fears, we forget and neglect the only One who can truly help us through our fears. The goodness and faithfulness of God pierce even the most unruly and unnerving fears. God has given us His Word, chronicling stories of His faithfulness and instructing us in the way forward. And He has promised us His presence, withholding no good thing from those who live with integrity (Psalm 84:11). When faced with the misconceptions we may have about God when we are afraid, we can remember who He is and what He has done. We may doubt God, reject His care, or question why He would allow fears to creep in. But when we consider the testimonies of God's faithfulness through the ages, we see He always cares for His people. He is the God who cared for us so much that He sent His only Son, Jesus, to live a perfect life on earth and die a sinner's death so that we could be reconciled to Him. Because of Jesus, we can combat our fears with hope for the ways God will use our circumstances for our good and His glory.

Praying to God, keeping our gaze on His purposes, meditating on His truths, and remembering His faithfulness are ways we combat fear. Each serves as a stepping stone to growing in greater knowledge and fear of the Lord. Our greatest means of combating our fears is possessing a great fear of God, loving and honoring Him as we were created to do.

The goodness and faithfulness of God

PIERCE EVEN THE MOST UNRULY AND UNNERVING FEARS.

In what ways can you utilize prayer to combat unruly fear in your life?

How does meditating on and memorizing Scripture shape our hearts and minds to deal with our fears?

Take some time to journal through what it would look like for you to grow in greater knowledge and fear of the Lord.

WEEK THREE

Day Two

CHRIST, OUR COMFORTER

SCRIPTURE: MATTHEW 11:28-30

When presented with biblical truths about how to handle our fears, we can sometimes depersonalize them. Even if we can acknowledge these truths intellectually, we might wrestle with planting these beliefs deeply in our hearts and souls. As we battle our fears, this can lead to a disconnect in who Jesus is and who we understand Him to be. We might readily understand Him as our Savior, accepting us through the gospel-saving work of salvation. We might even expectantly look to our future glory with Jesus when we will be like Him and dwell with Him. But we may struggle to connect with who Jesus is in the in-between.

Who is Jesus amid our fears? Who is He when we are anxious and afraid? Who is Jesus when we struggle to walk forward in faith? Who is Jesus when we look to self-protection or when we succumb to the pressures fear brings? We might be tempted to believe Jesus is only present when we are at our best and most deserving of a relationship with Him. We might assume we can only approach Him when we have cleaned ourselves up. But the Bible speaks to the truth of who Jesus is to us in every moment.

We find a beautiful portrait of His heart in Matthew 11:28-30. Jesus says, "Come to me, all of you who are weary and burdened, and I will give you rest. Take up my yoke and learn from me, because I am lowly and humble in heart, and you will find rest for your souls. For my yoke is easy and my burden is light." Jesus invites us to come to Him so that we might find rest for our souls, and how does He invite us to do so? He does not ask that we come to Him with fearless strength or with confidence and courage. The only qualifier for coming to Christ is that we are weary and burdened. He invites us when we have absolutely nothing to offer. And He delights in receiving us.

This speaks volumes to the person of Jesus. The work of the gospel reminds us that while we were still ungodly, sinful, and enemies of God, Christ died for us. He died for us at our absolute worst. Such a sacrificial display is only possible through a love more powerful and supernatural than anything we have ever known. A love that moved Christ from heaven to earth so He could save us from our sins. A love that is humble, gentle, and selfless. A love that bears all. And a love that continues to bring Christ near when our spirits are crushed and our souls are downcast. Christ calls us to Him in love because He knows our deepest needs are met in Him, and He will stop at nothing to remind us of this.

When we come to Christ, He offers us rest. This is not a one-time transaction. It is not only offered when we respond to the gospel in search of hope outside of this world. Nor is it only offered as eternal rest when we enter into heaven's gates. This rest is present and readily available to us. It is a rest that combats the swirling thoughts of worry and fear. It is a rest that surrounds us with solace when life feels frightening. When we find no comfort or peace within ourselves, it is a rest that remains firmly planted in the sovereign promises of God. We must continually seek the Lord for rest in a fear-filled world.

In our continual pursuit, Jesus is never exhausted by our need for rest in Him, and He never will be. When we think our fears are too much for Jesus, we gravely misunderstand who He is. Who better and more willing to carry and combat our fears than the One who took the sins of the world upon Himself? Time and time again, He has proven that He is more than capable of caring for us. In His essence, He is One who moves near to His people in love. He is compassionate and merciful when He considers the sin and struggles of His people. This does not negate His judgment but reminds us that His natural inclination is to act humbly and mercifully. Judgment is the last lever because mercy is the first. Likely, our greatest obstruction to receiving the grace and mercy offered to us in Christ is our own misunderstanding of who He truly is.

So, who is Jesus amid our fears? Scripture abounds with reminders of the Savior who offers Himself to His people in humility and love. He is everything He promised He would be. He is readily available to receive us (John 6:37), regardless of the fears we bring with us. He is the source and perfecter of our faith (Hebrews 12:2), using every single opportunity—even our fears—to shape us into His likeness. He is our advocate (1 John 2:1), rising to defend us in our failings based on the merits of His suffering and death. He is our peace (2 Thessalonians 3:16), bringing calm amid the waves and winds of a threatening world. He is our hope (1 Peter 1:3-4), piercing through even our deepest and darkest fears to a bright and glorious new morning. He is so much more than our words can say; we cannot attempt to exhaust the truth of who He is to us. Christians, be assured, we are best equipped to battle our fears with Jesus Christ.

We are best equipped

TO BATTLE OUR FEARS WITH JESUS CHRIST.

In what ways are you naturally inclined to think of Jesus amid your fears? How does Matthew 11:28-30 affirm or refute those thoughts?

What does Jesus promise when we come to Him? In what ways might we create obstacles for ourselves in coming to Him with our truest thoughts and fears?

Scripture abounds with reminders of who our Savior is. Adding to the passages presented in the study, take time to identify three passages of Scripture that tell us who Jesus Christ is to His people.

WEEK THREE

Day Three

PERFECT LOVE CASTS OUT FEAR

SCRIPTURE: I JOHN 4

When we lack fear of the Lord, we find ourselves too concerned with ourselves and other people, and we are robbed of true identity and lasting joy. Sin manipulates and tempts us to direct our worship and allegiance elsewhere. Maybe that looks like people-pleasing to avoid the uneasy feeling of disapproval. Maybe it looks like keeping a tight grip of control to avoid the unknown and uncertainty of our circumstances. Maybe it looks like covering up our sin to avoid the consequences. However it looks in the unique scenarios of our lives, sin promises false comfort and false security. It tricks us into believing God cannot protect, strengthen, and uphold us when we are afraid. Sin leads us to misdirect our gaze away from God and replace it with a faulty god on the throne of our hearts.

When we succumb to the fear of man, we idolize ourselves and people for what we think they can give us. What could we desire so much from people? Love and acceptance are some of our heart's greatest desires. The search for love and acceptance apart from God becomes an endless cycle of living to please others. Even if temporarily satisfying, it will never lead us to a place of hope and fulfillment. It will always leave us searching for more, and we will likely lose ourselves in the process. But more so, it will lead us in pursuit of something we can never attain. Man can fully accept us. Mankind does not have the power to do so, and when we place such an expectation on another sinful and limited person, they will always fail us.

The only One with the true power to perfectly love and approve of us once and for all is God. He has offered us full and final validation and acceptance through His Son, Jesus Christ. No man can offer this to us. First John 4 reminds us that God's love is revealed to us through the sacrificial gift of His Son to destroy the sin that separated us from the Father. It is only through Jesus's life, death, and resurrection that we can stand approved before a Holy God. God desires a loving relationship with us, and proper fear of the Lord is born out of a recognition of His astounding love for us. His love is compassionate, gracious, impartial, eternal. We could do nothing on our own to receive it or earn it. Instead, God lavishes His love freely upon us, based on His character and not our own. How different this is from the love of people!

We may be able to impress or win the affections of people, but we cannot impress God. God's love is humbling. At the height of our pride, we want gratification for our best efforts. But the gospel reminds us we have nothing to bring to the table of our salvation but our sin. We have no reason to boast. It is sheerly by God's grace that we are recipients of His love. Likewise, how freeing it is to know that in the same way we cannot earn God's love, we cannot lose God's love. His promises proclaim He will be faithful to His people, because of His great love for us, to the end of the ages.

When we rest in the perfect love of God, we can turn from fearing man because perfect love drives out fear (1 John 4:18). The love of God gives us purpose, security, fulfillment, and eternal acceptance. Loving and honoring God is a long and continual work. So, we should not grow weary when the fear of man continues to taunt us. Instead, we must run to and rest in the love of God, reorient our gaze to His purposes, and rejoice in His sovereign wisdom and care. We should regularly repent when we fall into man's snare and continually seek the Lord, that He may complete His work in us. He can use anything to shape us into His likeness. God fills us up with the love we so deeply desire, and it changes us.

God's love toward us is so comforting and transformative that it not only changes us and our relationship with Him but also changes our relationship with others. With the knowledge of God's abundant grace, how can we act with anything less than love toward others? If God has already accepted us in Christ, why would we still need acceptance from others? When our gaze is reoriented to the love of God, we no longer look to people for acceptance and approval. Instead, we are spurred to love others so that they are pointed to the only One who can offer them complete acceptance: Jesus Christ.

GOD'S LOVE TOWARD US IS SO *comforting and transformative* THAT IT NOT ONLY CHANGES US AND OUR RELATIONSHIP WITH HIM BUT ALSO CHANGES OUR RELATIONSHIP WITH OTHERS.

In what ways might you be prone to people-pleasing?

How does the fear of man expose our desire for love and acceptance?

How does the love of God speak to your deepest fears? How can you find comfort in the truth of His great love for you?

WEEK THREE

Day Four

FREEDOM TO LOVE AND SERVE

SCRIPTURE: GALATIANS 5:13-14

When our fears lead us to idolize people, we become glorified people-pleasers. People-pleasing is a full-time job, and it is exhausting. It is a round-the-clock pursuit of forgoing our true needs and opinions to appease and be accepted by those around us. It breeds superficiality and leaves little room for genuine and authentic relationships. It seeks to obtain the best thoughts and opinions of others, with little regard to what God thinks. When people-pleasing becomes second nature, we have given people too much precedence and power in our lives.

But the gospel sets us free from people-pleasing as we find our true worth and identity in Jesus Christ. When we feel secure in our relationship with Jesus, we will not manipulate or use people to feel secure. When we find purpose in Jesus, we will not place unrealistic expectations on our relationships to make us feel worthy and valuable. When we find fulfillment in Jesus, we can serve others without needing to take and consume. When Jesus is seated on the throne of our hearts, we are freed to enjoy people without being completely dependent on them. People will fail us, but Jesus is our perfect companion and comfort. Living in light of this truth opens the door for grace-filled, gospel-saturated relationships.

When the fear of man does not take precedence in our lives, we are freed to love and serve our brothers and sisters the way God created us to. After all, Scripture tells us, "For the whole law is fulfilled in one statement: Love your neighbor as yourself" (Galatians 5:14). God's love is costly in that He sent His Son to suffer and die on the cross to display it to us. Therefore, we can take big risks in our relationships with others. We can offer an invitation even when we do not receive one. We can affirm and encourage even when we do not see affirmation and encouragement reciprocated to us. We can forgive and offer grace with no strings attached. We can protect, comfort, and bless others, not merely to receive love but to reflect the love of God. We are freed to do all these things because, as Christians, we find our anchor in the firm foundation of God's love and acceptance through Jesus, and nothing can shake it. We can pour ourselves out with love and service because we are fulfilled in Christ.

Re-orientating our hearts toward God helps us to see the true gift and value of others. We were created to love people—not fear them. Loving and serving others does not mean always saying yes, being really nice, telling people what they want to hear, or doing what people want us to do. Those things can sometimes serve as a mask for the fear of man. They may seem harmless, but they can lead us into the same cycle of people-pleasing. Loving and serving others sometimes means doing and saying things that may not be well-received. We may have to say no to good things. We may need to point out a truth someone does not want to hear. We may need to call out a sin someone wants to keep hidden, or we may be called to act in other unpopular but fruitful ways.

We are equipped to live this way only by looking to the sacrifice of our Savior. As the incarnation of God Himself, Jesus Christ holds more freedom than we could possibly imagine—but He did not use His freedom as an opportunity for the flesh. He did not consider equality with God as something to be exploited. "Instead he emptied himself by assuming the form of a servant, taking on the likeness of humanity. And when he had come as a man, he humbled himself by becoming obedient to the point of death—even to death on a cross" (Philippians 2:5-8). Scripture calls us to follow His example. As we do so, we learn to trust in Him more deeply.

To love in such a God-centric way, we need the discernment, power, and wisdom that comes from Christ alone. We need discernment because it can be challenging to know exactly what loving others should look like in every circumstance. We need the power of the Holy Spirit at work in us because on our own we are incapable of loving like Christ. We need wisdom and help from God's Word and from God's people to help us honor God in the way we love others. Whether friends, enemies, believers, non-believers, neighbors, or family, the goal for our treatment of others is to love and serve them in ways that speak to the heart of Christ. We love because Christ first loved us and gave Himself up for us (1 John 4:19). The love of Christ completely and thoughtfully shapes Christian love. It brings us freedom from the fear of man, so we can serve and love man.

THE LOVE OF CHRIST
completely and thoughtfully
SHAPES CHRISTIAN LOVE.

How can the fear of man keep you from loving others well? What examples have you seen of this in your own life?

How does God's foundational love free you to love and serve others, even if you do not receive their love and service in return?

How can you practically display the sacrificial love of Jesus in your home? In your church? In your workplace? In your neighborhood?

WEEK THREE

Day Five

WALKING IN THE FEAR OF THE LORD

SCRIPTURE: PROVERBS 2:1-6

The Bible encourages Christians to walk in the fear of the Lord, live in reverent awe, and worship Him. But do we fear God just because we are instructed to fear Him? Do we fear God simply to replace our fear of man? No, because there are greater things at stake—the glory of God. God created us to enjoy and worship Him in His presence. And He is worthy of our worship. He is merciful and majestic, powerful, sovereign, and holy. Our fear of Him leads us to revel in His supreme and surpassing greatness. He is worthy of our greatest affections and deepest praises.

Our fear of Him brings glory to His name. In the same way that we stand on the top of a mountain and look in awe at the grand beauty that surrounds us, we glorify God when we are in wondrous awe of Him and His work. We glorify God when we rightly love others instead of fearing them. In John 13:34-35, Jesus says, "I give you a new command: Love one another. Just as I have loved you, you are also to love one another. By this everyone will know that you are my disciples, if you love one another." With a Christ-centered love for people, we bear witness to a watching world that it is worth giving our lives to Jesus.

Jesus is worth living for, and blessings abound when we walk in the fear of the Lord. It changes everything about the way we live and love. It changes our marriages because our worth and value are no longer placed in our spouses. It changes our church involvement because we serve and give ourselves, not to receive something in return. It changes our friendships because we can invite others into our lives as our true selves. It changes how we think about our days, future plans, safety, comforts, and everything that leaves us prone to fear. No rejection or exposure or harm can rob us of the joy of God's presence. This truth gives us unshakable confidence for the rest of our days.

The gospel is the answer to all of our doubts and insecurities, our crippling anxieties, our longings for love and acceptance, and every fear that misdirects our gaze from God.

Fear tempts us to run to ourselves and others, unveiling what we cling to most to meet our needs. But we must fight to remember who God is and what He has done. We have a God who sought us out in love and sacrificed His own righteous Son for our sin so that, through salvation, we could stand faultless before His throne. We have no need to respond as Adam and Eve responded in the garden—running and hiding from Him. God sets us free from shame and fear through the saving work of the gospel. We are not left to hide behind fig leaves, but instead, we are invited to hide in the shadow of His wings. We find no gain in directing our fear and awe elsewhere. God is the One who sees and knows us completely (Psalm 139:1). He is our greatest defense and our greatest help (Psalm 18:2). He guards our hearts and protects our desires. He offers us true safety and security. God promises us His presence in this life and the next.

In Christ, the hope of glory shatters the substance of our fears. We are too loved to be left relying and depending on someone or something that will inevitably fall and crumble under the weight of our needs. All of our needs are met in Him. All of our fears are comforted by Him. All of our desires are kept by Him. As He carries us safely and securely through this life, He is preparing a place for us in His kingdom—a place where we will be overcome with peace the moment we enter into it. God will fully and finally restore all things. Our fears will melt away. Our joy will overflow. Our praises will ring loud! Our hearts will rest secure, and we will never know the fear of this world again. We will only walk in perfect peace and joy with God and His people forever.

While we wait and prepare for that glorious day, we are to live unto the glory of God in reverent fear of Him. We must choose to live each day, not to be consumed by our own selfish wants and desires, not to attain worldly affirmations, not to please people, not to rest comfortably and safely in our own little corner of the world, not to safeguard ourselves against rejection, and not to isolate ourselves. Rather, we are to display the glory of God in everything we do. We are equipped to put to death our misplaced fears. With the Holy Spirit's help, God's people to walk with us, God's Word to teach us, and Jesus to sanctify us, we can faithfully walk in the fear of the Lord.

God promises us His presence

IN THIS LIFE AND THE NEXT.

How does true reverence and fear of the Lord change everything about our lives?

What cultivates your awe and worship of God? How can you continually cultivate it?

What did you learn about yourself regarding your fear of man and your fear of God throughout this study?

What is your greatest takeaway from this study, and how do you plan to apply it to your life?

SCRIPTURE

Memory Verse

"COME TO ME, ALL OF YOU WHO ARE WEARY AND BURDENED, AND I WILL GIVE YOU REST. TAKE UP MY YOKE AND LEARN FROM ME, BECAUSE I AM LOWLY AND HUMBLE IN HEART, AND YOU WILL FIND REST FOR YOUR SOULS. FOR MY YOKE IS EASY AND MY BURDEN IS LIGHT."

MATTHEW 11:28-30

Week Three Reflection

REVIEW ALL PASSAGES FROM THE WEEK

Summarize the main points from this week's Scripture readings.

What did you observe from this week's passages about God and His character?

What do this week's passages reveal about the condition of mankind and yourself?

How do these passages point to the gospel?

How should you respond to these passages? What specific action steps can you take this week to apply them in your life?

Write a prayer in response to your study of God's Word. *Adore God for who He is, confess sins He revealed in your own life, ask Him to empower you to walk in obedience, and pray for anyone who comes to mind as you study.*

WHEN I AM AFRAID...

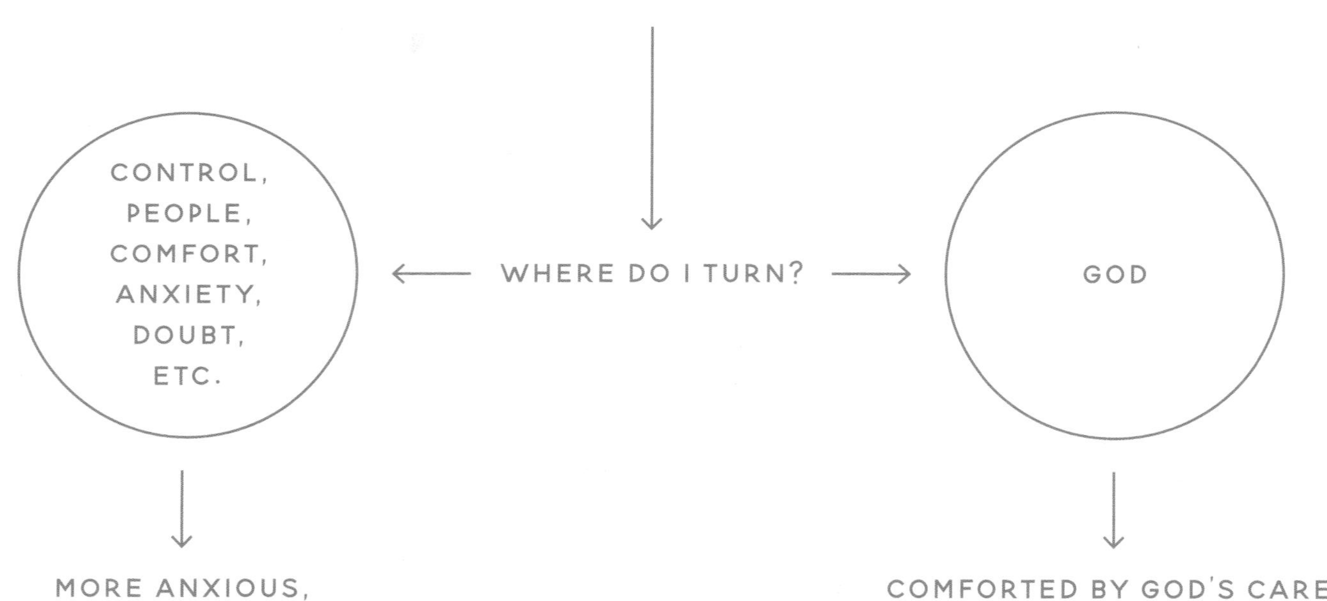

WITH THE HOLY SPIRIT'S HELP,
GOD'S PEOPLE TO WALK WITH US,
GOD'S WORD TO TEACH US,
AND JESUS TO SANCTIFY US,
we can faithfully walk in the fear of the Lord.

What is the gospel?

THANK YOU FOR READING AND ENJOYING THIS STUDY WITH US! WE ARE ABUNDANTLY GRATEFUL FOR THE WORD OF GOD, THE INSTRUCTION WE GLEAN FROM IT, AND THE EVER-GROWING UNDERSTANDING IT PROVIDES FOR US OF GOD'S CHARACTER. WE ARE ALSO THANKFUL THAT SCRIPTURE CONTINUALLY POINTS TO ONE THING IN INNUMERABLE WAYS: THE GOSPEL.

We remember our brokenness when we read about the fall of Adam and Eve in the garden of Eden (Genesis 3), where sin entered into a perfect world and maimed it. We remember the necessity that something innocent must die to pay for our sin when we read about the atoning sacrifices in the Old Testament. We read that we have all sinned and fallen short of the glory of God (Romans 3:23) and that the penalty for our brokenness, the wages of our sin, is death (Romans 6:23). We all need grace and mercy, but most importantly, we all need a Savior.

We consider the goodness of God when we realize that He did not plan to leave us in this dire state. We see His promise to buy us back from the clutches of sin and death in Genesis 3:15. And we see that promise accomplished with Jesus Christ on the cross. Jesus Christ knew no sin yet became sin so that we might become righteous through His sacrifice (2 Corinthians 5:21). Jesus was tempted in every way that we are and lived sinlessly. He was reviled yet still yielded Himself for our sake, that we may have life abundant in Him. Jesus lived the perfect life that we could not live and died the death that we deserved.

The gospel is profound yet simple. There are many mysteries in it that we will never understand this side of heaven, but there is still overwhelming weight to its implications in this life. The gospel tells of our sinfulness and God's goodness and a gracious gift that compels a response. We are saved by grace through faith, which means that we rest with faith in the grace that Jesus Christ displayed on the cross (Ephesians 2:8-9). We cannot save ourselves from our brokenness or do any amount of good works to merit God's favor. Still, we can have faith that what Jesus accomplished in His death, burial, and resurrection was more than enough for our salvation and our eternal delight. When we accept God, we are commanded to die to ourselves and our sinful desires and live a life worthy of the calling we have received (Ephesians 4:1). The gospel compels us to be sanctified, and in so doing, we are conformed to the likeness of Christ Himself. This is hope. This is redemption. This is the gospel.

SCRIPTURES TO REFERENCE:

GENESIS 3:15	*I will put hostility between you and the woman, and between your offspring and her offspring. He will strike your head, and you will strike his heel.*
ROMANS 3:23	*For all have sinned and fall short of the glory of God.*
ROMANS 6:23	*For the wages of sin is death, but the gift of God is eternal life in Christ Jesus our Lord.*
2 CORINTHIANS 5:21	*He made the one who did not know sin to be sin for us, so that in him we might become the righteousness of God.*
EPHESIANS 2:8-9	*For you are saved by grace through faith, and this is not from yourselves; it is God's gift—not from works, so that no one can boast.*
EPHESIANS 4:1-3	*Therefore I, the prisoner in the Lord, urge you to walk worthy of the calling you have received, with all humility and gentleness, with patience, bearing with one another in love, making every effort to keep the unity of the Spirit through the bond of peace.*

Thank you for studying God's Word with us

CONNECT WITH US

@thedailygraceco
@dailygracepodcast

CONTACT US

info@thedailygraceco.com

SHARE

#thedailygraceco

VISIT US ONLINE

www.thedailygraceco.com

MORE DAILY GRACE

The Daily Grace App
Daily Grace Podcast